ENDANGERED AND THREATENED ANIMALS

THE KOALA

A MyReportLinks.com Book

Carl R. Green

MyReportLinks.com Books

an imprint of

Enslow Publishers, Inc.

Box 398, 40 Industrial Road
Berkeley Heights, NJ 07922
USA

MyReportLinks.com Books, an imprint of Enslow Publishers, Inc. MyReportLinks is
a trademark of Enslow Publishers, Inc.

Library of Congress Cataloging-in-Publication Data

Green, Carl R.
  The koala / Carl R. Green.
     p. cm. — (Endangered and threatened animals)
Summary: Discusses what koalas are, why they are endangered, what their
current status is, and what is being done to help them. Includes
Internet links to Web sites related to koalas.
Includes bibliographical references (p.   ).
  ISBN 0-7660-5058-0
  1. Koala—Juvenile literature. 2. Endangered species—Juvenile
literature. [1. Koala. 2. Endangered species.] I. Title. II. Series.
  QL737.M384 G74 2003
  599.2'5—dc21

                                   2002008995

Printed in the United States of America

10 9 8 7 6 5 4 3 2 1

To Our Readers:
Through the purchase of this book, you and your library gain access to the Report Links that specifically back
up this book.
The Publisher will provide access to the Report Links that back up this book and will keep these Report Links
up to date on **www.myreportlinks.com** for three years from the book's first publication date.
We have done our best to make sure all Internet addresses in this book were active and appropriate when we
went to press. However, the author and the Publisher have no control over, and assume no liability for, the
material available on those Internet sites or on other Web sites they may link to.
The usage of the MyReportLinks.com Books Web site is subject to the terms and conditions stated on the
Usage Policy Statement on **www.myreportlinks.com**.
A password may be required to access the Report Links that back up this book. The password is found on the
bottom of page 4 of this book.
Any comments or suggestions can be sent by e-mail to comments@myreportlinks.com or to the address on
the back cover.

Photo Credits: Australian Koala Foundation, p. 34; © Australian Museum, 2003, p. 29; © Corel
Corporation, pp. 3, 11, 35, 36; © Friends of the Koalas, pp. 15, 32; © National Geographic Society,
p. 24; © 1996, webStories, Inc., p. 16; © 2002 Wild Scenes, p. 13; Enslow Publishers, Inc., p. 38;
Hunter Koala Preservation Society, p. 23; John Bavaro, p. 19; Liz Hunter, pp. 1, 26;
MyReportLinks.com Books, p. 4; 1997 Office of Polar Programs, p. 12; Photo courtesy of Lone Pine
Koala Sanctuary, Brisbane, Australia, www.koala.net, pp. 18, 28, 40, 41; Wildcare: The Koala Page,
pp. 21, 27.

Cover Photo: © Corel Corporation

Contents

MyReportLinks.com Books
Great Books, Great Links, Great for Research!

MyReportLinks.com Books present the information you need to learn about your report subject. In addition, they show you where to go on the Internet for more information. The pre-evaluated Report Links that back up this book are kept up to date on **www.myreportlinks.com**. With the purchase of a MyReportLinks.com Books title, you and your library gain access to the Report Links that specifically back up that book. The Report Links save hours of research time and link to dozens—even hundreds—of Web sites, source documents, and photos related to your report topic.

Please see "To Our Readers" on the Copyright page for important information about this book, the MyReportLinks.com Books Web site, and the Report Links that back up this book.

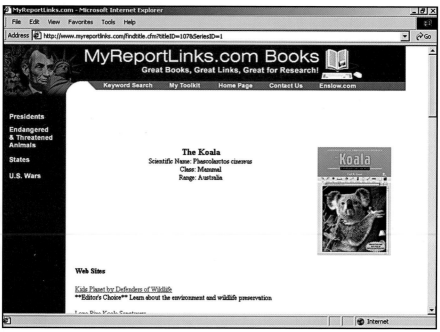

Access:

The Publisher will provide access to the Report Links that back up this book and will try to keep these Report Links up to date on our Web site for three years from the book's first publication date. Please enter **EKL6258** if asked for a password.

The Internet sites described below can be accessed at
http://www.myreportlinks.com

*EDITOR'S CHOICE

▶ **Kids Planet by Defenders of Wildlife**
Electronic fact sheets on over fifty species of wildlife, including the
koala, are presented by region. You will also find the "Defend It!"
section that shows different ways of helping defend wildlife and
the environment.

Link to this Internet site from http://www.myreportlinks.com

*EDITOR'S CHOICE

▶ **Lone Pine Koala Sanctuary**
Can koalas swim? Find out by reading the "Frequently Asked
Questions" section. Learn about how the first and largest koala
sanctuary in the world works to preserve the wildlife of Australia.
Do not miss the Live Webcam section!

Link to this Internet site from http://www.myreportlinks.com

*EDITOR'S CHOICE

▶ *National Geographic* **Creature Feature—Koala**
Can you believe a newborn koala is the size of a jellybean? That is
tiny! Read about this and other "Fun Facts" while visiting *National
Geographic*'s Creature Feature—Koala. View the map that shows
where koalas live, and send a postcard to a friend!

Link to this Internet site from http://www.myreportlinks.com

*EDITOR'S CHOICE

▶ **Friends of the Koalas**
"Koala Facts" will give you general information about the koala as
well as facts about its diet, breeding, and problems. Learn how this
organization is trying to prevent koala deaths from habitat loss, dog
attacks, and cars. Photos included.

Link to this Internet site from http://www.myreportlinks.com

*EDITOR'S CHOICE

▶ **Australian Koala Foundation**
The Australian Koala Foundation provides you with information
about threats to koalas, their habitat, and ways you can help save these
animals. Listen to the sound a koala makes by visiting the "All About
Koalas" section.

Link to this Internet site from http://www.myreportlinks.com

*EDITOR'S CHOICE

▶ **Koalas**
On the San Diego Zoo Web site you will find a general introduction
to the koala. You will also learn about the koala's diet, habits, and
legal status.

Link to this Internet site from http://www.myreportlinks.com

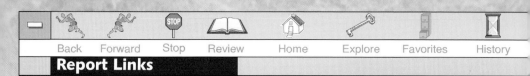

Report Links

The Internet sites described below can be accessed at
http://www.myreportlinks.com

Animal World

This site offers current news, views, and issues about animals and the preservation of habitat in Australia. Learn about the Foster Care program and what Australians are being asked to do if an injured or sick animal is found.

Link to this Internet site from http://www.myreportlinks.com

Australian Aboriginal Art

To Australian Aborigines, "the Dreaming" is much more than a few dreams left over from a night's sleep. At this site, read essays that explain, "the Dreaming," and see the beautiful Aboriginal art that tells its history.

Link to this Internet site from http://www.myreportlinks.com

Australian Conservation Foundation

The Australian Conservation Foundation is a group that fights to preserve the environment. Current issues that could hurt the koala include radioactive dump plans, the impact of mining on the environment, and land clearing.

Link to this Internet site from http://www.myreportlinks.com

Australian Indigenous Population

Learn about the Aborigine people and their history. Read about how they have formed "outstations" to move away from larger settlements to renew links with nature and continue to hunt, gather, and live in dwellings as they did before European settlement.

Link to this Internet site from http://www.myreportlinks.com

Australian Museum Online

The extensive research and collections section of this site provides many facts on a wide range of animals. Also read about earth sciences and environmental sciences. Fascinating information on a variety of topics can be found in the "Features" section.

Link to this Internet site from http://www.myreportlinks.com

Endangered Species

The Endangered Species Web site provides information about endangered species all over the world. Here you will find the endangered species list, a list of conservation organizations, facts about species, the texts of laws and policies, and much more.

Link to this Internet site from http://www.myreportlinks.com

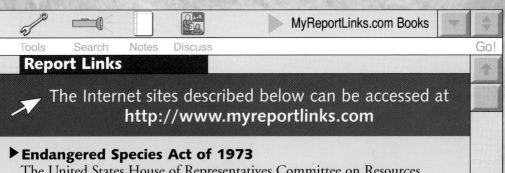
Report Links

The Internet sites described below can be accessed at
http://www.myreportlinks.com

▶ **Endangered Species Act of 1973**
The United States House of Representatives Committee on Resources
Web site contains the complete text of the Endangered Species Act
of 1973.

Link to this Internet site from http://www.myreportlinks.com

▶ **Environment Australia**
Environment Australia brings you information on Australia's
biodiversity, international issues, environmental protection laws, and
other topics. Find out what invasive species are, and view beautiful
photos of Australia.

Link to this Internet site from http://www.myreportlinks.com

▶ **Fact Sheet: Koala**
Do koalas socialize with each other? How big are they when they are
born? Find answers to these and other questions while viewing some
breathtaking photos. The "Animal Bytes" section offers more interesting
facts on the koala.

Link to this Internet site from http://www.myreportlinks.com

▶ **Friends Of Local Koalas Land And Wildlife**
Read a speech given by the Secretary of FOLKLAW at the Australian
Koala Foundation Conference in 1997. Learn about the various
methods proposed as ways to control the koala population on
Australia's Mornington Peninsula.

Link to this Internet site from http://www.myreportlinks.com

▶ **Hunter Koala Preservation Society, Inc.**
This Society works to preserve the koala. Learn interesting facts and
statistics related to the rescue calls they have received. Do not miss the
"Koalas in Care" section to see pictures and read updates on the
condition of these rescued koalas.

Link to this Internet site from http://www.myreportlinks.com

▶ **Koala**
At this Web site you will find an interesting diagram of the koala's
body. You can also learn about the koala's life cycle, including its habits,
anatomy, and diet.

Link to this Internet site from http://www.myreportlinks.com

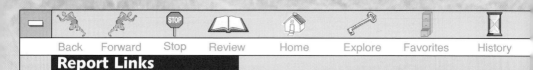

Report Links

The Internet sites described below can be accessed at
http://www.myreportlinks.com

The Koala Page
This site provides an interesting look at the koala and its habitat. View beautiful photos and a chart of the eucalyptus trees that koalas favor as housing and feeding stations.

Link to this Internet site from http://www.myreportlinks.com

Lower Blue Mountains Koala Survey
Do you know what koala signs and tracks look like? This site shows you! Read about this project, which researched koala habitat and presence in the Lower Blue Mountains of Australia.

Link to this Internet site from http://www.myreportlinks.com

Marsupial CRC
Marsupials are both wonderful and problematic. Read about research on the conservation and management of marsupials. Learn about research on fertility control as an answer to the controversial idea of culling.

Link to this Internet site from http://www.myreportlinks.com

Marsupials at Fort Worth Zoo
Want to see pictures of the koala, kangaroo, and other marsupials? These pictures are from the Fort Worth Zoo in Texas. Information and facts about the animals accompany each picture. If you have time, sneak a peak at the other animals at the zoo, too!

Link to this Internet site from http://www.myreportlinks.com

The Marsupial Museum
Fifteen marsupials are featured at this virtual museum. View photos, and read interesting facts about each one. Not only can you learn about koalas, you also can learn about other interesting animals, such as the Tasmanian devil.

Link to this Internet site from http://www.myreportlinks.com

National Science Foundation
The National Science Foundation's Office of Polar Programs offers a wealth of information on polar sciences. The "Polar Research Support" section has many links to information about little-known places such as Antarctica and Gondwanaland.

Link to this Internet site from http://www.myreportlinks.com

Report Links

The Internet sites described below can be accessed at
http://www.myreportlinks.com

▶ Perth Zoo
Did you know that the koala's conservation status is "Threatened?"
Visit the Perth Zoo in Australia and learn about this beautiful animal.
Be sure to check out the "Births and New Arrivals" section for some
great photos!

Link to this Internet site from http://www.myreportlinks.com

▶ Tell me about: Australia
Here you will find information about Australia's geography, history,
animals, education, and people. Learn about the flora and fauna while
viewing photos of the land down under.

Link to this Internet site from http://www.myreportlinks.com

▶ Wildcare—The Koala Page
Learn about the anatomy of the koala at this veterinarian-made
site. Scientific information accompanies both the photos and the
illustrations. Read about the research being done on leukemia in koalas.

Link to this Internet site from http://www.myreportlinks.com

▶ WIRES
What exactly is a bilby? Learn all about this long-eared marsupial in
WIRES's extensive section of Australian animals. Find out what
programs are set in place to help sick and injured wildlife, including
the koala.

Link to this Internet site from http://www.myreportlinks.com

▶ World Wildlife Federation
The World Wildlife Federation is a global organization that works to
preserve the earth from destruction. See what this organization is doing
to help save wildlife. You can also select Australia and other country-
specific sites to see what is happening all over the world.

Link to this Internet site from http://www.myreportlinks.com

▶ Victoria's Three Great Zoos
Meet all of Australia's wildlife while visiting this site, which spotlights
all three of Victoria's zoos. At the Melbourne Zoo site you can learn
about the Victorian koala and see beautiful photos.

Link to this Internet site from http://www.myreportlinks.com

Scientific Name
Phascolarctos cinereus (P.c.).
There are three subspecies, found only in Australia:
　P.c. *victor* (Victoria)
　P.c. *cinereus*
　　(New South Wales)
　P.c. *adustus* (Queensland)

Class
Mammalia

Sub-Class
Marsupialia

Family
Phascolarctidae

Closest Relative
Ground-dwelling wombat.

Current Habitat
Eucalyptus forests and woodlands of eastern and south-central Australia.

Size and Weight
At birth, .5 inches long,
　less than .5 ounces (14 g);
Adult males, 24–30 inches
　(61–76.2 cm) long,
　16–30 lbs. (7.3–13.6 kg);
Adult females, 16–24 inches
　(40.6–6 km) long,
　12–18 lbs (5.4–8.2 kg).

Diet
Up to 2.5 pounds (1.1 kg) of eucalyptus leaves each day. The leaves also provide the koala with most of the water it needs.

Sleeping Habits
Koalas sleep up to 20 hours a day and feed mainly at night. Their sleeping habits help conserve energy.

Current Population
Estimates place the national population as low as 100,000, down from around 12 million.

Current Status
Threatened within many parts of the species' remaining geographic range.

Life Span
In the wild, up to 10–12 years. In sanctuaries, up to 20 years.

Greatest Threat To Survival
80 percent of original forest habitat has been destroyed.

Legislative Status
Conservation efforts vary from state to state in Australia. The koala is officially listed as "vulnerable" in New South Wales under that state's *Threatened Species Conservation Act 1995*.

*Figures represent average measurements.

Lovable Australians

Look up there, in the tree—it is a monkey!
No, that has got to be a sloth!
Hold on, I am pretty sure it is a small bear!
Sorry, you are all wrong. This is Australia—the island continent. The furry animal clinging to the top of that tall eucalyptus tree is a koala. Like its homeland, this amazing animal has a long and colorful history.

▶ Geography Played a Role

About 45 million years ago, in the earth's southern hemisphere, a supercontinent, known as Gondwanaland gradually broke apart. The drifting landmasses formed modern-day South America, Antarctica, Africa, India, New Zealand—and Australia. Some 170 species of marsupials evolved in Australia's forests, woodlands, shrublands, and grasslands. North America, by contrast, is home to only one marsupial—the opossum. The offspring of all

Many people think the koala is a bear. ▶ Naturalists, however, class the koala as a marsupial. Its closest relative in North America is the opossum.

marsupials are born at a very early stage of development and generally continue their growth inside the *marsupium* —the mother's "pouch." The females of some marsupial species develop a temporary pouch during the breeding season. Other species never develop a pouch. The subclass *Marsupialia* (marsupials) includes four orders: carnivorous marsupials; bandicoots and bilbies; the marsupial mole; and macropods (kangaroos and wallabies), possums, wombats, and the koala.

The koala's fossil record dates back some 15 million years and includes at least twelve extinct koala species. One

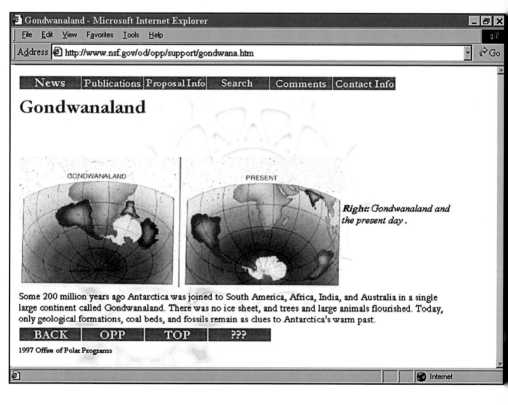

▲ Australia separated from Gondwanaland about 160 million years ago. The period of isolation that followed allowed for a unique mix of wildlife to evolve on the island continent. Koalas, therefore, are found only in Australia.

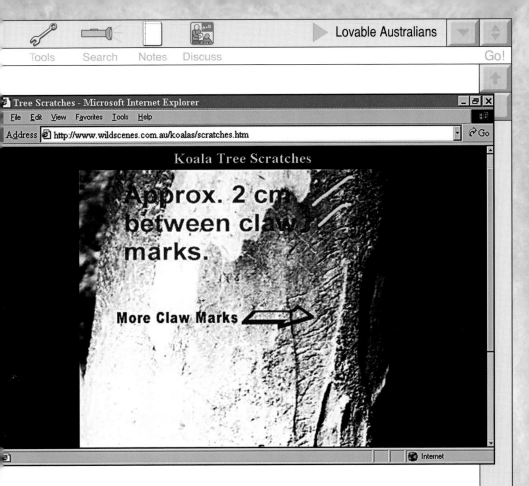

Tree Scratches - Microsoft Internet Explorer

File Edit View Favorites Tools Help

Address http://www.wildscenes.com.au/koalas/scratches.htm   Go

Koala Tree Scratches

Approx. 2 cm between claw marks.

More Claw Marks ⟹

Internet

▲ *The sharp claws of the koala leave distinctive scratches on the bark of some trees, including this much-favored eucalyptus.*

early species grew to around twice the size of today's largest males. The earliest koala species appear to have lived in rainforests, which covered much of the Australian continent at that time. It is thought likely that as the climate became drier and rainforests receded, eucalypts (Australian evergreen trees) became more prominent. Koalas then adapted to the drier forests and woodlands. Stone-Age Aborigines arrived on the continent some sixty thousand years ago. Today, the name *Aborigines* refers to the descendants of those original settlers.

Naming the Koala

Each Aboriginal tribal group that lived near koalas gave the furry tree-dweller a different name. One group called it the *cullawine*. Others knew it as the *koolewong*, the *colo*, the *koolah*, the *boorabee* . . . and the *koala*.[1] English settlers arrived in the late 1700s. Some dubbed the gentle creature the *bangaroo* or *native bear*. In time, they settled on koala, a word that means "no drink." In fact, koalas do sometimes drink water, particularly during times of drought. Mainly they rely on the moisture found in the leaves they eat to keep themselves hydrated.

The koala intrigued the scientists who came to study Australia's wildlife. The fuzzy-eared animals lived in eucalyptus trees and ate the leaves. Like the kangaroo and the wombat, the females carried their young in a pouch. Scientists studied the clues and gave the koala a flawed scientific name: *Phascolarctos cinereus.* The name translates as "ash-colored pouched-bear."[2] The reference to the pouch is correct, but koalas can also be brownish in color—and bears belong to a far different group of mammals than do koalas and other marsupials.

Legends of the Koala

Like all hunters and gatherers, the Australian Aborigines use stories to explain the workings of the natural world. Their treasury of legends often is referred to as *The Dreaming,* or *Dreamtime.* Creation stories explain how Earth came to be and why the seasons change, and they tell of the way of life of the Spirit Ancestors. Other tales describe the origins of plants and animals and teach young people to know and respect the natural world.

Tools   Search   Notes   Discuss   Go!

Friends of the Koalas - Koala Facts - Microsoft Internet Explorer

File   Edit   View   Favorites   Tools   Help

Address 🔁 http://home.vicnet.net.au/~koalas/facts.html   ↗Go

THE LITTLE AUSTRALIAN PHILLIP ISLAND WOULD HATE TO LOSE

FRIENDS OF THE KOALAS INC.

Welcome
News
About Us
Koala Watch
Koala Facts
How to Help
Membership
Contact Us

Koala Facts

General – Diet – Breeding – Problems

General

- Is the koala a bear?
- How long do koalas live?
- How large are koalas?
- What are the koala's natural predators?
- Do koalas have territories?
- Do koalas build shelters or nests?
- How do koalas spend their time?
- Where are koalas naturally found?
- Are koalas indigenous to Phillip Island?

Internet

▲ *According to an Aboriginal legend, the first koala was once a young boy who hid in a tree.*

What does Aboriginal mythology tell us about the origins of the koala? In one legend a family of Aborigines adopt an orphan boy, but refuse to share their precious water with him. When he asks for food and drink, they feed him eucalyptus leaves. One day, the boy climbs a tree and hides his family's water pots in the branches. As he sings a magical song, the tree grows taller and taller. When the people return, they coax him down from the tree. Then the angry men beat him with sticks. As the blows rain down, the boy's body becomes thicker and sprouts a dense coat of fur. The beating has turned him into a koala!

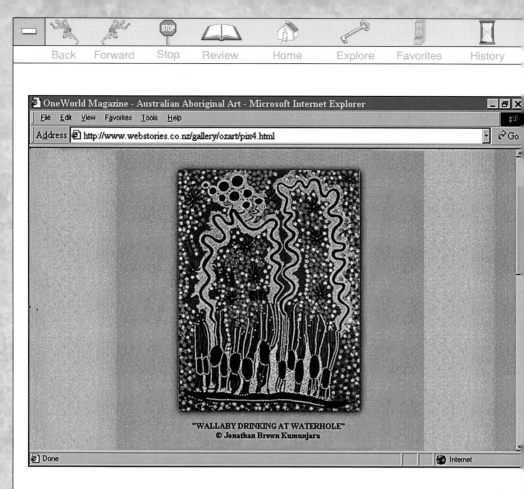

▲ The Aborigines used different forms of art, including dance, music, and paintings, to pass on their stories. This painting, called "Wallaby Drinking at Waterhole," depicts the story of the South Australian hare-wallabies.

The koala boy tries to escape by climbing the magic tree, but the men chop it down. The water pots spill and the water is lost. In the confusion, the koala boy flees to the forest, leaving the tribe to suffer through a long drought.

The legend teaches respect for the koala. The Aborigines may roast and eat a koala, but they must not break its bones. If they do not show the proper respect, the koala boy will send a new drought to punish them.[3]

The Koala's Changing World

The English settlers who swarmed into Australia in the 1800s did not believe in Aboriginal legends. Intent on taming the wilderness, they cleared the land and hunted the koala for its fur. Over time, approximately 80 percent of the koala's eucalyptus forests were lost.[4] In 1919 alone, hunters slaughtered more than one million koalas in the state of Queensland.[5] While koalas are now protected, habitat clearing for development and agriculture, forest fires, and disease have added to the number lost in recent years. Conservationists estimate that the national koala population, which once numbered in the millions, has now fallen to a few hundred thousand.

Most people love these gentle, cuddly-looking creatures. Indeed, businesses use the koala's appealing "teddy bear" looks to sell everything from airline tickets to boot polish. Reports that the koala is in danger inspire cries of "Save the koala!" The first step in saving this unique animal, scientists urge, is taking action to protect its habitat. However, before we can appreciate why it is vital to save the koala, it would be helpful to understand what makes this Australian native so special.

Chapter 2 ▶

The Koala's Lifestyle

Almost everyone loves the koala. The obvious appeal is not hard to understand. Here are some typical comments made by tourists as they wander through Australia's Lone Pine Koala Sanctuary.

"There's a momma and her joey," says one, pointing upward. "They're so cute!"

"Yes," agrees her friend. "They really do look like living teddy bears."

"Let's get closer," whispers a third visitor. "I want to cuddle that little one."

At that point, a keeper is likely to remind the tourists that koalas only look cuddly. Beneath that thick fur is a strong, agile body. When angry or fearful, koalas defend themselves with their sharp teeth and claws.

▶ Family Features

The koala "look" features a handsome face with wide-set brown

Koalas look very soft and cuddly. However these usually-gentle animals can be dangerous when they are angry or scared.

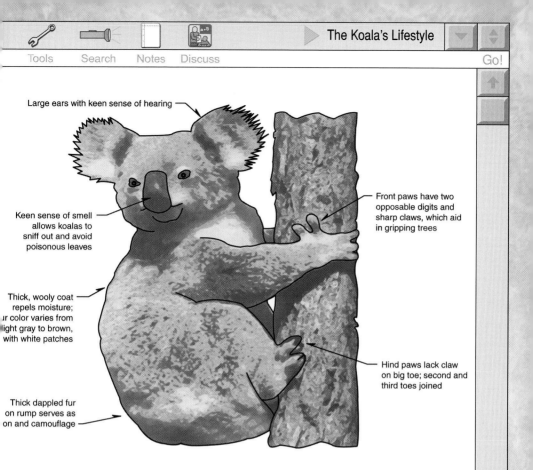

Large ears with keen sense of hearing

Keen sense of smell allows koalas to sniff out and avoid poisonous leaves

Thick, wooly coat repels moisture; ur color varies from light gray to brown, with white patches

Thick dappled fur on rump serves as on and camouflage

Front paws have two opposable digits and sharp claws, which aid in gripping trees

Hind paws lack claw on big toe; second and third toes joined

eyes, fuzzy, erect ears, and a large, black nose ideally suited to picking up the scents of the bush (the Australian wilderness). The male's call is a loud, snorting bellow. Females and babies make softer clicking and squeaking noises to each other. When injured, a koala's scream can be mistaken for that of a human baby.

Scientists tell us that *Phascolarctos cinereus* has three "subspecies," each found in a different state. Queensland's koalas, having evolved in the region's warmer climate, have short, light-gray coats and are smaller than southern koalas. The koalas of New South Wales tend to be gray or gray-brown. Victoria has the coldest winters and the largest koalas—as large as twice the size of their northern cousins. The Victorian koalas have shaggy, dark-gray coats

and the fluffiest ears of all three subspecies. In all three groups, males generally grow to be much larger than the females. The largest southern males tip the scales at more than thirty pounds.[1]

A Life in the Treetops

On the ground, the koala usually moves slowly and somewhat awkwardly. To climb, the koala grasps a tree trunk with its front paws and pushes upward with its muscular rear legs. The front paws, each with its two opposable digits, or "thumbs," are ideal for grasping branches and picking leaves. The rear paws have a single, clawless hallux, or "thumb," and four clawed toes. Like other marsupials, two of the clawed toes are partly fused to form a grooming claw.

The koala feeds, sleeps, and mates in the treetops. On a typical day, it may stay awake for four or five hours and sleep for up to twenty. At times it hangs upside down, swinging by one strong front paw. Although the koala prefers to move carefully from branch to branch, it is quite capable of leaping. Koalas occasionally make mistakes. If they fall, they usually manage to land safely.

Koalas are capable short-distance swimmers when the need arises. They take to the water mostly to escape predators or to reach new food sources. Sadly, some koalas drown each year in backyard swimming pools. After falling into the pools, they are unable to climb out.

Unlike most tree-dwelling mammals, koalas do not have an obvious tail. Scientists explain that the koala's ground-dwelling ancestors did not need tails. The Aborigines, by contrast, say that the first koalas did have tails. In one of their legends, the other animals suspect that Koala has caused a drought. To gather proof, they send Lyrebird to spy on him. Lyrebird soon spots Koala hanging

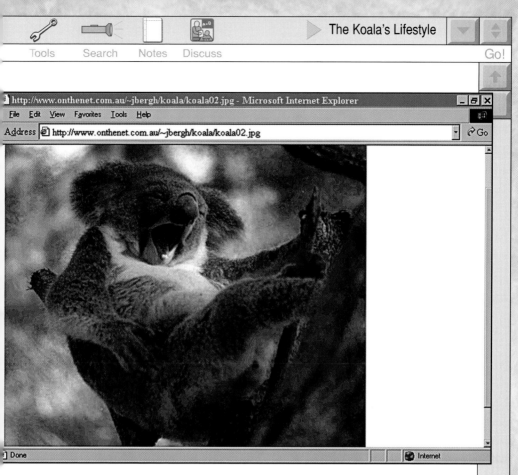

http://www.onthenet.com.au/~jbergh/koala/koala02.jpg - Microsoft Internet Explorer

File   Edit   View   Favorites   Tools   Help

Address http://www.onthenet.com.au/~jbergh/koala/koala02.jpg   Go

Done   Internet

▲ Koalas spend most of their time in the treetops of eastern and south-
central Australia, feeding and sleeping.

by his tail, drinking from a hidden spring. Angered by this
selfish behavior, Lyrebird sets fire to the tree. Koala is
forced to beat a hasty retreat—and leaves his tail behind.[2]

▶ Eating Habits of a Folivore

Unlike grass-eating herbivores, *folivores* feed on leaves,
bark, and buds. Koalas feed mainly on the foliage of eucalyptus trees (also known as gum trees). Australia is home to
hundreds of species of eucalyptus, but koalas prefer a select
few for their main food source in each given area or
region.[3] When food is scarce, koalas will sometimes eat the
leaves of trees such as forest oak and brush box.

An adult koala consumes up to two and one-half pounds (1.13 kg) of eucalyptus leaves each day. No matter how thoroughly the koala chews each mouthful, the leaves are difficult to digest. The koala's intestine has adapted to cope with its diet. The secret lies in the *caecum,* a storage area leading from the small intestine. Here, bacteria convert cellulose (plant fibers) into carbohydrates that the body can absorb. Stretched out, a koala's caecum would measure roughly eighty inches (203.2 cm) in length.[4]

Along with being hard to digest, eucalyptus leaves contain toxic chemicals. *Cineole,* for example, would kill most other mammals, but it does not harm the koala. At certain times of the year, some gum trees also produce *hydrocyanic acid.* Koalas avoid this danger by checking the scent of each leaf they pick. They discard leaves that contain high levels of poison.

Koalas drink water so rarely that people once thought they did not need water. The koala does require water, but leaves and dew supply almost all of its needs. Reportedly, koalas occasionally eat a few mouthfuls of earth. Experts believe the soil is likely to provide much-needed minerals. Their leafy diet, with its strong-smelling oils, gives koalas a distinct odor. Some people say they smell like cough drops!

▶ Raising a Joey

It is January, a hot, summer day in Australia. Deep in the forest, the loud bellow of a male koala echoes through the trees. Soon a female responds with a call of her own. She finds the male by sniffing the sharp, musky scent he used to mark his territory, or home range. In mating season, the scent flows from a gland on his chest. After climbing into his tree, the female leads the male on a noisy chase through the branches, often accompanied by bouts of biting and

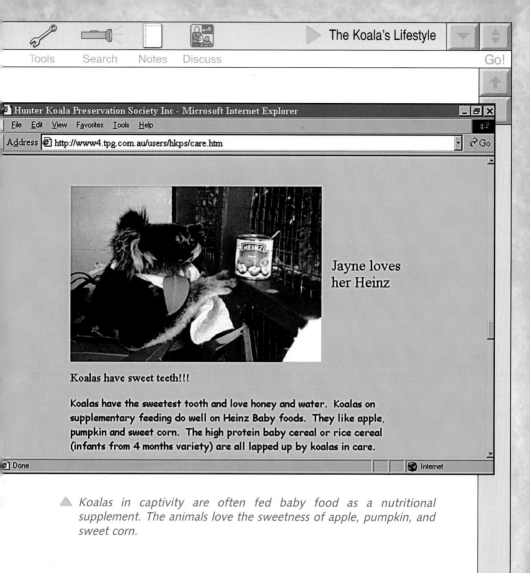

Jayne loves
her Heinz

Koalas have sweet teeth!!!

**Koalas have the sweetest tooth and love honey and water. Koalas on
supplementary feeding do well on Heinz Baby foods. They like apple,
pumpkin and sweet corn. The high protein baby cereal or rice cereal
(infants from 4 months variety) are all lapped up by koalas in care.**

*Koalas in captivity are often fed baby food as a nutritional
supplement. The animals love the sweetness of apple, pumpkin, and
sweet corn.*

clawing. The chase ends when she is ready to mate. Mating
may occur within an area where the two koalas' territories
overlap. Otherwise, the female returns to her own home
range after mating.[5]

About thirty-five days later, the female gives birth. To
prepare, she sits upright and wedges herself into a fork of her
home tree. Soon a pink, hairless baby koala, or joey, emerges
from her birth canal. Driven by instinct and pulling itself
along by its strong front limbs, the jellybean-sized baby
begins the climb to its mother's pouch. The pouch is located

in the center of her abdomen. Once inside the pouch, the young koala attaches to one of the female's two teats. As it nurses, the teat swells inside the newborn's mouth. Over the next few months, almost nothing can shake it loose.

At around six months, the joey is roughly seven inches (17.78 cm) long and fully furred. It kicks the sides of the pouch and peeks out now and then. When it does venture outside, it hurries back to the pouch at the first sign of danger. At around five or six months of age, the joey feeds on "pap," a soft, green feces produced by the mother. The pap contains bacteria the joey's intestine will

A joey lives in its mother's pouch for about six months, or until it grows too large. At this point, the joey clings to its mother's back when she travels.

need to enable it to digest a high-fiber diet of potentially toxic eucalyptus leaves.[6] The joey puts its head outside the pouch to feed, stretching the opening of the pouch down toward the source of the pap. This is why koalas sometimes appear to have a backward-facing pouch.

Out On Its Own

Soon the joey begins to nibble on young eucalyptus leaves. Before long, it has grown too large to fit in the pouch. At feeding time, it pushes its head inside to nurse. When the female moves about, the joey clings to her back. By the following summer, the youngster is nearly weaned. At this stage, some joeys go off on their own; others remain within the mother's home range until they are a little older. Young males seem to travel farther than young females. Often, young males leave during the mating season after being chased off by an adult male. If they survive to the age of four, they will be ready to fight for their own home range.

Threats to Survival

A cartoon from Kookaburra Productions says it all. A forlorn koala stands next to the sawed-off stump of a giant eucalyptus tree. "Y'know," he says, "I can barely recognize my childhood home these days. We used to live in a high rise."[1]

The koala's tree very likely fell victim to a logger's chainsaw. Eucalypts have been cut down to clear the land for homes, roads, or factories, as well as for their lumber, oil, and gum. Even today, Australia's remaining eucalyptus forests face a similar threat. Instead of living in protected national parks, most koalas live on land that is privately owned. Efforts to protect wildlife often clash with the property owners' desire to develop the land. As a result, the threat posed by loss of habitat is as real as the threat from poachers who shoot koalas for their pelts.

The koala's habitat is disappearing as bulldozers clear the forests to make room for farms, roads, and houses.

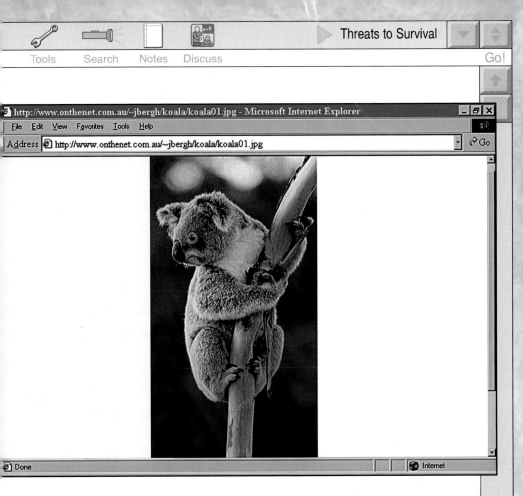

File Edit View Favorites Tools Help

Address http://www.onthenet.com.au/~jbergh/koala/koala01.jpg

▲ *Habitat loss has played a major role in the koala's decline. Without the protection of quiet woodlands, the animals are exposed to noise, traffic, and domestic dogs. This stressful environment often brings on disease, making the threat even more dire.*

▶ The Era of the Hunters

Before Aborigines reached Australia, koalas flourished in the forests and woodlands. As the Aboriginal population grew, more and more koalas were killed for food. In that long ago era, koalas inhabited southwestern Australia as well as the eastern coastal and inland regions. Over time, the koalas vanished from the Southwestern region of the continent.[2]

Aborigines treated the koala with respect, even when roasting it for supper. It was forbidden, for example, to skin

the animal before cooking it. The Europeans who arrived in the late 1700s did not share the same reverence for living things. In 1810, George Perry described the koala as having "a clumsy, awkward appearance," with "little . . . to interest the naturalist."[3]

By the end of the 1800s, the world market for furs was increasing. Koala pelts were warm, and slow-moving koalas were easy game. The hunters went to work. A one-month season in 1927 produced 584,738 pelts. When koalas nearly disappeared from some regions, a public outcry arose. By the late 1930s, all of the Australian states had outlawed the hunting of koalas for food or fur.[4] Poachers, as usual, ignored the new laws. Stores sold koala pelts as wombat or possum.[5] Poaching did not cease to be a serious threat until the demand for pelts declined. Without buyers, the poachers turned to other game. For most Australians, however, their long romance with what may be the world's best-loved marsupial was just beginning.[6]

Loss of Habitat

The concept of living in harmony with nature has been slow to take root in the Western world. Most of the Europeans who settled in places like North America and Australia would have laughed at that ideal. In their minds, the land was

Koala sanctuaries were created so that the animals could live contently in their natural habitat.

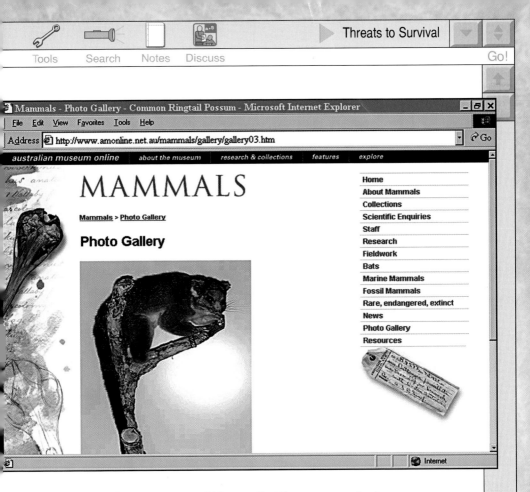

australian museum online   about the museum   research & collections   features   explore

MAMMALS

Mammals > Photo Gallery

Photo Gallery

Home
About Mammals
Collections
Scientific Enquiries
Staff
Research
Fieldwork
Bats
Marine Mammals
Fossil Mammals
Rare, endangered, extinct
News
Photo Gallery
Resources

Internet

Fur sellers sometimes told buyers that they were purchasing opossum furs when, in fact, the pelts were those of protected koalas.

meant to be used. They largely ignored the rights and the knowledge of the existing native peoples. In Australia, huge tracts of prime habitat, home to large numbers of native plants and animals, vanished. Hunters moved in with their guns and settlers cleared the land for farms and towns.

An estimated 80 percent of the eucalypt forests and woodlands have already been cleared for agriculture and development.[7] To make matters worse, the coastal areas favored by koalas are prized as housing sites. Even when patches of habitat are spared, the remaining koala population faces threats from cars, domestic dogs, and diseases brought on by stress.

When towns and traffic replace an old-growth forest, the impact on wildlife is devastating. Food supplies are lost along with habitat. Wild animals either move away or starve to death. Bewildered koalas sometimes climb telephone poles in a desperate search for their missing gum trees.

Hundreds of koalas also die each summer when wildfires race through their habitats. The shocked survivors are left to nurse burns that may later become infected. Fire-damaged eucalyptus trees sprout new growth—but the young leaves can be highly toxic. They also take several weeks to grow.

Fire is not the only danger to koalas living near urban areas. Towns that care about their wild neighbors put up "Caution—Koala Crossing" signs. The signs are reminders that animals never look both ways before crossing the road. Despite these warnings, several thousand koalas are killed each year by careless drivers.

Habitat losses can also result where eucalypts become highly stressed or diseased. For example, dieback, or leaf loss, commonly occurs when there has been extensive habitat disturbance. Trees also may suffer from infestations of sap-sucking insects such as *lerps* (or *psyllids*). The insects do their worst damage after habitat disturbance has reduced the number of birds that normally keep them under control.

▶ Predators and Disease

In undisturbed forests and woodlands, the koala has little to fear. Until settlers introduced dogs and foxes to Australia, koalas fell prey to only a handful of predators. High in the trees, joeys sometimes were snatched up by wedge-tailed eagles, owls, or pythons. Dingoes (wild native dogs) and goannas, a type of large native lizard, were the main threats when koalas ventured away from their trees. Today these natural predators still exist. In addition, pet dogs and their feral (wild) cousins kill thousands of koalas each year. While koalas have strong, agile bodies and sharp claws, they are no match for the powerful jaws of most dogs.

Koalas are luckier when it comes to coping with parasites. The oils that give them their "cough drop" odor repel fleas and some ticks—but not bacteria or viruses. One of the most serious diseases koalas suffer from is caused by the *Chlamydia* bacterium.[8] Many koalas in the wild carry chlamydia bacteria. However, symptoms may not develop until they become stressed, usually because of the loss of their habitat. Chlamydial infections can cause blindness, pneumonia, and infections of the genital and urinary tracts. The result is a condition known as "wet bottom," or "dirty tail," which leads to infertility in females.[9] Birth rates within stressed and diseased populations decrease as more females become infertile. Doses of antibiotics can control the disease, but only if rescuers find the sick animal in time. Koalas also are known to suffer from blood and skin cancers.

Disease does not rank as the koala's most critical problem. The greatest threat comes from humans. When a koala forest lies in the path of development, "progress" often carries the day. For many reasons, including economics, government often fails to consider the needs of wildlife. The solution is both simple and complex: People must make the sacrifices needed to save the koala. If they do not, the species will slip ever closer to extinction.

Save the Koala!

Legislation in New South Wales provides some hope of saving koala populations and providing for long-term recoveries. Nevertheless, habitat loss continues to occur throughout the koala's range. Koala groups and conservationists are doing their best to raise awareness about the growing danger. They point to enormous problems threatening the koala's survival and beg that steps be taken to

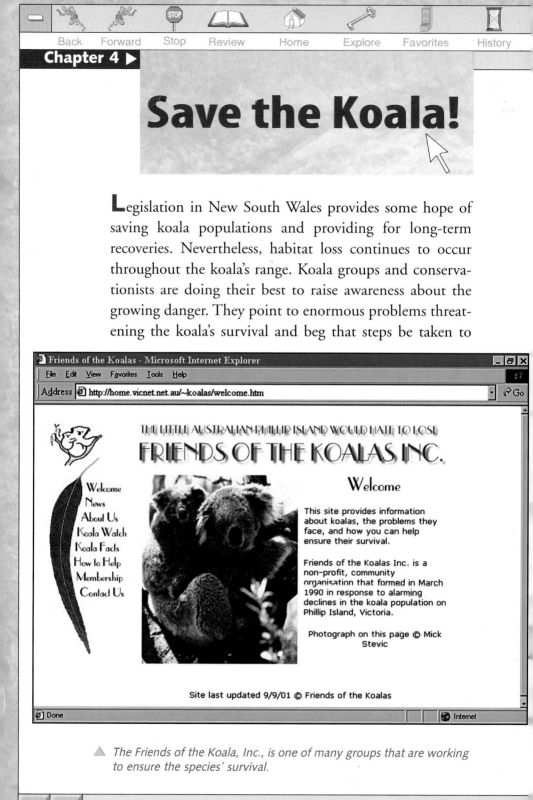

Friends of the Koalas - Microsoft Internet Explorer

File   Edit   View   Favorites   Tools   Help

Address http://home.vicnet.net.au/~koalas/welcome.htm

THE LITTLE AUSTRALIAN PHILLIP ISLAND WOULD HATE TO LOSE

FRIENDS OF THE KOALAS INC.

Welcome
News
About Us
Koala Watch
Koala Facts
How to Help
Membership
Contact Us

Welcome

This site provides information about koalas, the problems they face, and how you can help ensure their survival.

Friends of the Koalas Inc. is a non-profit, community organisation that formed in March 1990 in response to alarming declines in the koala population on Phillip Island, Victoria.

Photograph on this page © Mick Stevic

Site last updated 9/9/01 © Friends of the Koalas

Done   Internet

▲ The Friends of the Koala, Inc., is one of many groups that are working to ensure the species' survival.

save it. After all, they argue, koalas are an Australian national treasure. Studies show that these gentle animals attract some $1.1 billion to the Australian economy each year. Saving the koala and its habitat is not just humane. It also makes good economic sense.[1]

Protecting Habitat

Loving the koala is easy. Stretching that warm, fuzzy feeling to embrace the koala's habitat is another matter. With their specialized eating habits, koalas cannot live in just any type of woodland. Without a healthy eucalyptus forest and the right type of eucalypts to feed and shelter them, they must move away or die. In most Australian states where koalas live, laws protect them. Even so, there are few laws on the books that effectively protect their habitat. The future of the species depends largely on how well Australia deals with the issue of habitat protection.

The koala's human friends are helping with much-needed restoration efforts in some areas by planting eucalyptus trees. However, this is a gradual process. The plan needs a major government commitment of money and resources if it is to be effective.

What Is Being Done?

The struggle to save the koala has enlisted worldwide support. When concerned citizens band together to form groups, they can speak with a single, more powerful voice. Several groups are working hard to find solutions to the koala's problems and to alert the public to the dangers facing koalas. They use newspapers, television, and the Internet to spread the word.

Ensuring that koalas are safe in the future will require hard work, money, planning, and stricter law enforcement.

Organizations such as the Australian Koala Foundation are working hard to protect the koala.

On Phillip Island, in Eastern Victoria, a group called Friends of the Koalas (FOK) is doing its part. Each month, the group sponsors a Koala Habitat Day. Members meet at a koala reserve to plant trees, pull weeds, and do general cleanup. Some of the money the group raises goes to support Phillip Island Nature Park's Koala Conservation Centre. To cut back on road deaths, FOK posts warning signs and lobbies for lower speed limits.[2]

At the national level, the Australian Koala Foundation (AKF) is working on a number of initiatives. The AKF is compiling a national Koala Habitat Atlas that identifies koala habitat and describes the condition of each area. With the data in hand, the officials who make decisions about land use will be better able to consider the needs of the koalas and other wildlife. In the future, access to such information could prevent decisions like the one in Queensland, which led the state government to spend $6 million to buy land for a koala reserve. Unfortunately, the costly reserve, koala experts say, can support only thirty-five koalas.[3] The AKF is also working to persuade the Australian federal government to join the struggle. The foundation is urging lawmakers to pass laws that will protect the koala's habitat all across its range. Without strong national laws to safeguard these woodlands, the koala's future remains in jeopardy.

Zoos and Hospitals Play a Part

In California, the San Diego Zoo has bred and displayed koalas since the 1950s. To feed its fussy guests, the zoo grows gum trees in its nearby

Volunteers are trained ▶ to take care of sick and injured koalas.

wild animal safari park. The San Diego Zoo also lends koalas to zoos in Chicago, Cleveland, and Toronto, among other cities. To repay the loans, some zoos support koala conservation groups such as the Australian Koala Foundation. In addition, the visitors who flock to these exhibits walk away with a new respect for the koala and its needs. Every effort that increases awareness and encourages support—financial and otherwise—gives the koala a better chance at survival.

In Australia, trained volunteers give "hands-on" care to sick and injured koalas. The Koala Preservation Society of New South Wales runs the koala hospital in Port Macquarie. The hospital began its work by taking in three tiny joeys in the early 1970s. One joey died, but Cubby and Tiny Tim survived. As land development continued unchecked, the hospital expanded to care for the increasing numbers of koalas affected by habitat loss. Workers planted more than twelve thousand trees to feed their sick, injured, and orphaned patients. Each morning, a work crew collects the day's supply of leaves. Staff members take

In order to ensure the koala's survival, everyone must do his or her part to help.

motherless joeys home with them. These orphans need—
and receive—around-the-clock care.[4] Even so, many joeys
die. The koala hospital near Brisbane in Queensland treats
some twelve hundred koalas a year. Only about 250
survive to be returned to the wild.[5]

Management Planning for Koalas

Koala support groups generally agree on a six-step plan to
protect koalas. The steps include:

- Identifying and protecting the trees and habitat
koalas must have to survive.

- Allowing koala populations to live undisturbed
by providing adequate buffer zones around
their habitats wherever possible.

- Maintaining corridors between habitats that
allow for the safe movement of young koalas
between breeding groups.

- Restoring habitats and habitat corridors to allow
for long-term recovery of koala populations.

- Managing traffic threats by not building new
roads in important koala habitat areas and by
lowering speed limits in key areas.

- Employing tighter controls on pet dogs and
better management of feral dogs.

Taking action to protect the koala is not just the
responsibility of scientists and koala groups. Everyone,
from politicians to park rangers, developers, farmers, and
homeowners, must join in the effort.

Protecting Australia's Earth Spirit

The threat to the koala's future is not unique. Wildlife biologist Walter Reid reports that at least twenty species of the world's mammals have become extinct since 1900. Today, 25 percent of the remaining species of mammal are threatened, as well as 34 percent of all fish.[1]

Will the koala eventually become one of the species that becomes extinct in the wild? In the natural world, species do perish. Sad to say, our own species has speeded up the process. However, the koala and other threatened animals need not vanish. If humans are the cause, they can also be the solution.[2]

▼ Koalas are only native to Australia. Most of them are found in the Australian states of South Australia, Queensland, New South Wales, and Victoria.

Present Status in South Australia

The koala was hunted to extinction in South Australia by the mid-1920s. Later, a new population of koalas was transported to South Australia from Victoria. Today, koalas are clinging to an uncertain existence on Kangaroo Island and in the Adelaide Hills, where their official listing is "rare and vulnerable."[3]

Victoria

Having survived near-extinction during the years of the fur trade, the state's koala population is holding its own. Here, as in other regions of Australia, koalas are living in scattered habitats. Victoria has no listing for its koalas. As a result, decisions about land use do not always address the koalas' needs.

New South Wales

This state, which has lost much of its eucalyptus forests, officially lists the koala as "rare and vulnerable." Koalas can be found in fragmented habitats along the coastline. Towns such as Port Macquarie and Lismore take pride in caring for their colonies of "suburban" koalas. Even so, further land development—and bushfires—could tip the balance against the state's koalas.[4]

Queensland

This state is thought to be home to Australia's largest koala population. In 1995, Queensland downgraded the status of its koalas from "protected" to "common."[5] Ann Sharp of the Australian Koala Foundation argues that these koalas are "sitting on a time bomb." The state's laws favor land clearing, and forests and woodlands are falling all across the state. Sometimes a town tries to stop a builder from

▲ Australian laws still permit the destruction of koala habitat. Without protection, the species may soon become extinct.

cutting down the trees its koalas need to survive. If the town wins its case, a state law allows the builder to sue for loss of income. All too often, the koala is the loser.[6]

What Does the Future Hold?

"Koalas feared dead in Australia fires," the headline says. The report describes the "black Christmas" fires that raced through the forests of New South Wales late in 2001. Unable to flee, thousands of koalas may have died when their trees burst into flames. Wildlife experts worry that the fires left the state's koalas in more danger than ever.[7] An outsider might argue that these uncontrolled fires have always been a part of the Australian landscape. Today, however, the fact that many koala populations are living in isolated and fragmented pockets of woodland increases the fires' deadly effect.

The Australian Koala Foundation believes that the large-scale destruction of koala habitat can be halted—or at least slowed. The crucial problem, the foundation argues, is that 80 percent of the nation's koalas live on privately-owned land. Therefore, laws are needed that will encourage Australian landowners to protect the koala habitat that lies on their properties. Deborah Tabart, the AKF's executive director, proposes a National Koala Act with four main goals:

- To focus on the protection and restoration of koala habitat on a national level, as well as the protection of the animals themselves.

- To use financial and other incentives to encourage landowners to conserve habitat.

The koala is a much-loved animal that would be sorely missed if it became extinct.

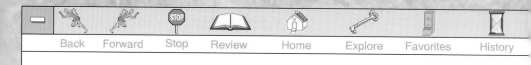
- To set up a national koala recovery program.
- To act as a model for future laws that protect all endangered native species.[8]

▷ Ensuring A Secure Future

Pushing new laws through Australia's parliament will require a strong commitment from lawmakers, as well as a show of public support. Only with the help and support of koala-lovers around the world will the Australian Koala Foundation achieve its vision of ensuring a secure future for this unique and much-loved animal.

According to Ken Phillips of the Koala Preservation Society of New South Wales, it is important to ensure "the continued survival of this very special earth spirit. When the last member of a species disappears, so, too, does a part of the earth and a part of each of us."[9]

We cannot afford to let that happen.

This series is based on the Endangered and Threatened Wildlife list compiled by the U.S. Fish and Wildlife Service (USFWS). Each book explores an endangered or threatened animal, tells why it has become endangered or threatened, and explains the efforts being made to restore the species' population.

The United States Fish and Wildlife Service, in the Department of the Interior, and the National Marine Fisheries Service, in the Department of Commerce, share responsibility for administration of the Endangered Species Act.

In 1973, Congress took the farsighted step of creating the Endangered Species Act, widely regarded as the world's strongest and most effective wildlife conservation law. It set an ambitious goal: to reverse the alarming trend of human-caused extinction that threatened the ecosystems we all share.

The complete list of Endangered and Threatened Wildlife and Plants can be found at

http://endangered.fws.gov/wildlife.html#Species

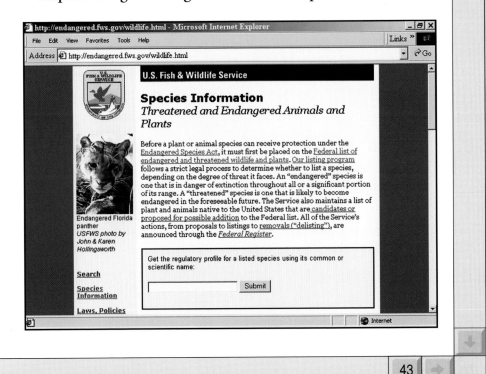

Chapter 1. Lovable Australians

1. Ann Sharp, *The Koala Book* (Gretna, La.: Pelican Publishing Co., 1995), p. 22.

2. Simon Hunter, *The Official Koala Handbook* (London: Chatto & Windus, 1987), pp. 13–14.

3. Ibid., pp. 20–21.

4. Sharp, p. 22.

5. Australian Koala Foundation, "History of the Koala," *All About Koalas*, n.d., <http://www.savethekoala.com/history.html> (January 9, 2002).

Chapter 2. The Koala's Lifestyle

1. Simon Hunter, *The Official Koala Handbook* (London: Chatto & Windus, 1987), pp. 26–27.

2. "Koala," *Native Symbols—A Guide to the Energies of the Australian Bush,* n.d., <http://www.newage.com.au/library/native-symbols.html> (February 2, 2002).

3. Hunter, p. 28.

4. Ann Sharp, *The Koala Book* (Gretna, La.: Pelican Publishing Co., 1995), pp. 37–38.

5. H. D. Williamson, *The Year of the Koala* (New York: Charles Scribner's Sons, 1975), pp. 32–34.

6. Hunter, p. 49.

Chapter 3. Threats to Survival

1. Ann Sharp, *The Koala Book* (Gretna, La.: Pelican Publishing Co., 1995), p. 114.

2. Anthony Lee and Roger Martin, *The Koala: a Natural History* (Kensington, NSW Australia: New South Wales University Press, 1988), pp. 24, 78.

3. Sharp, p. 100.

4. Ibid., p. 106.

5. Lee and Martin, pp. 83–84.

6. "Threats," *Information on Koalas, Australian Koala Foundation.* n.d., <http://www.savethekoala.com/koala/> (February 2, 2002).

7. H. D. Williamson, *The Year of the Koala* (New York: Charles Scribner's Sons, 1975), p. 88.

8. Lee and Martin, p. 86.

9. "Threats." Australian Koala Foundation.

Chapter 4. Save the Koala!

1. Australian Koala Foundation, n.d., http://www .savethekoala.com/koala/ (February 2, 2002).

2. "FOK Initiatives," *Friends of the Koalas,* September 9, 2001, <http://home.vicnet.net.au/~koalas/initiatives.html> (March 2, 2002).

3. Ann Sharp, *The Koala Book* (Gretna, La.: Pelican Publishing Co., 1995), p. 122.

4. Ken Phillips, *Koalas: Australia's Ancient Ones* (New York: Macmillan, 1994), pp. 66–75.

5. Deborah Tabart, "My Week," *Grist Magazine,* September 2000, <http://www.gristmagazine.com/grist/ week/tabart091100.stm> (February 2, 2002).

Chapter 5. Protecting Australia's Earth Spirit

1. Quoted in Katie de Koster, *Endangered Species* (San Diego, Calif.: Greenhaven Press, 1998), p. 22.

2. Virginia Morell, "The Sixth Extinction," *National Geographic,* February 1999, <http://www .nationalgeographic.com/ngm/9902/fngm/index.html> (March 21, 2002).

3. "The Koala—Endangered or Not?" *Australian Koala Foundation,* June 1998, <http://www.savethekoala.com/ danger.html> (January 9, 2002).

4. Ann Sharp, *The Koala Book* (Gretna, La.: Pelican Publishing Co., 1995), p. 118.

5. "Media Release: National Koala Act Summit," *Australian Koala Foundation,* April 2001, <http://www.savethekoala.com/nka.html> (March 28, 2002).

6. Sharp, p. 116.

7. Emma Tinkler, "Koalas Feared Dead in Australia Fires," *PE.com,* January 2002, <http://www.pe.com/nationworld/worldstories/2002-0105-koalas.html> (March 2, 2002).

8. "Media Release: National Koala Act Summit," *Australian Koala Foundation.*

9. Ken Phillips, *Koalas: Australia's Ancient Ones* (New York: Macmillan, 1994), p. 148.

Further Reading

Bright, Michael. *Koalas.* New York: Gloucester Press, 1990.

Burt, Denise. *Koalas.* Minneapolis, Minn.: Lerner Publishing Group, 1999.

de Koster, Katie. *Endangered Species.* San Diego, Calif.: Greenhaven Press, 1998.

Feeney, Kathy. *Koalas for Kids.* Madison, Wis.: Turtleback Books, 1999.

Kalman, Bobbie. *The Life Cycle of a Koala.* New York: Crabtree Publishing Company, 2002.

Leach, Michael. *Koala: Habitats, Life Cycles, Food Chains, Threats.* Austin, Tex.: Raintree Publishers, 2002.

Lee, Anthony and Roger Martin. *The Koala: a Natural History.* Kensington NSW, Australia: New South Wales University Press, 1988.

Malaspina, Anna. *The Koala.* Farmington Hills, Mich.: Gale Group, 2002.

Phillips, Ben. *KOALAS: The Little Australians We'd All Hate to Lose.* Canberra: Australian Government Publishing Service, 1990.

Phillips, Ken. *Koalas: Australia's Ancient Ones.* New York: Macmillan, 1994.

Sharp, Ann. *The Koala Book.* Gretna, La.: Pelican Publishing Company, 1995.